POPULAR SONGS

HAL LEONARD
STUDENT PIANO LIBRARY

Spooky Halloween Tunes

Arranged by Fred Kern

T0081580

ISBN 978-1-4803-5270-4

HAL•LEONARD®
CORPORATION
7777 W. BLUEMOUND RD. P.O. BOX 13819 MILWAUKEE, WI 53213

Visit Hal Leonard Online at
www.halleonard.com

CONTENTS

Casper the Friendly Ghost

from the Paramount Cartoon

Words by Mack David
Music by Jerry Livingston
Arranged by Fred Kern

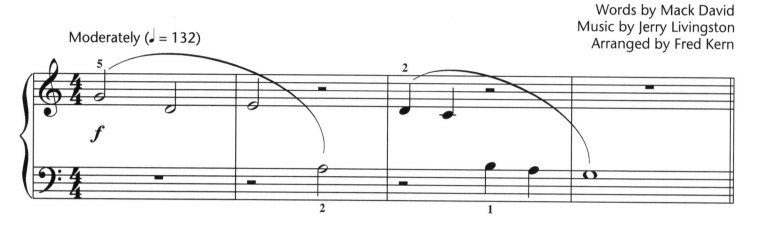

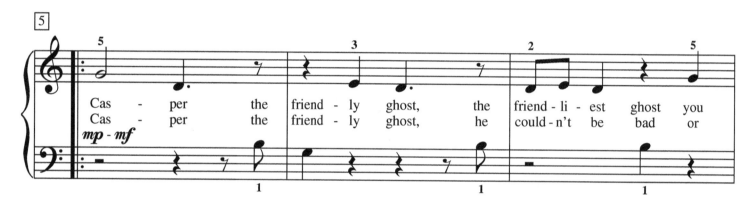

Cas - per the friend - ly ghost, the friend - li - est ghost you
Cas - per the friend - ly ghost, he could - n't be bad or

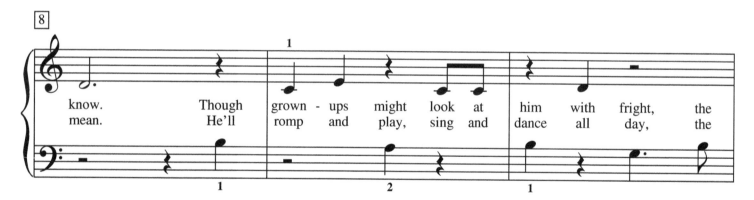

know. Though grown - ups might look at him with fright, the
mean. He'll romp and play, sing and dance all day, the

Accompaniment (Student plays one octave higher than written.)

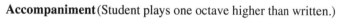

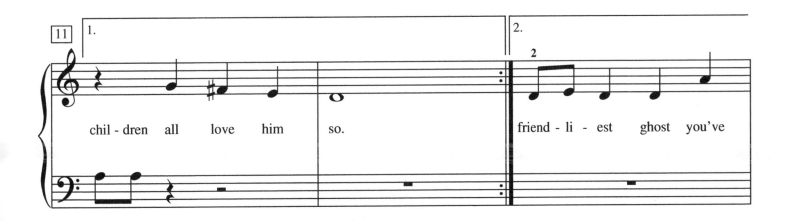

chil - dren all love him so. friend - li - est ghost you've

seen. He al - ways says "Hel - lo," and he's real - ly glad to

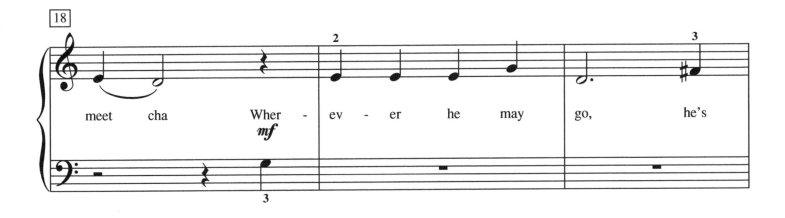

meet cha Wher - ev - er he may go, he's

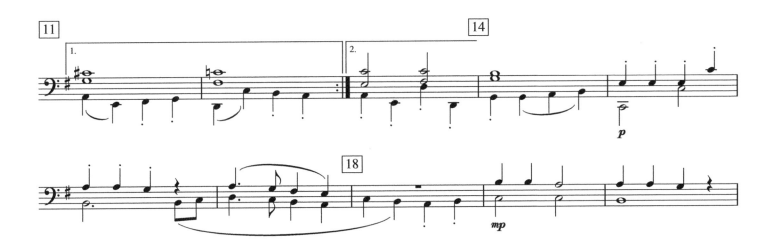

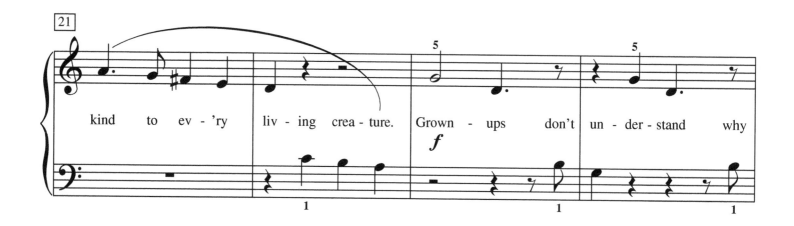

kind to ev - 'ry | liv - ing crea - ture. | Grown - ups don't un - der - stand why

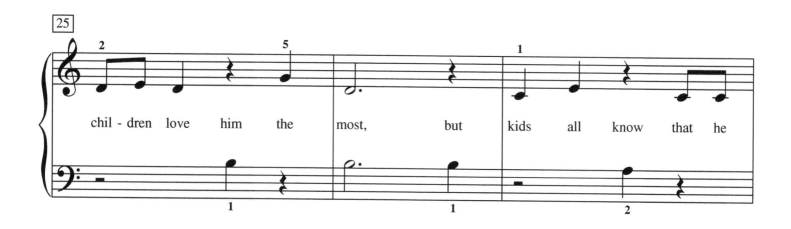

chil - dren love him the | most, but | kids all know that he

loves them so, | Cas - per the friend - ly | ghost.

Addams Family Theme

Theme from the TV Show and Movie

Music and Lyrics by
Vic Mizzy
Arranged by Fred Kern

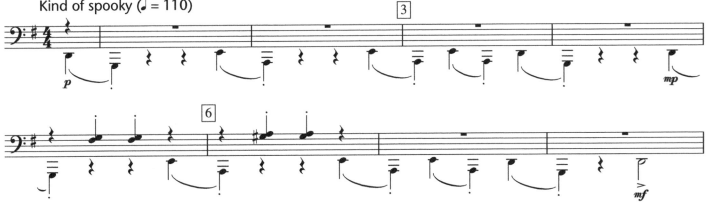

7

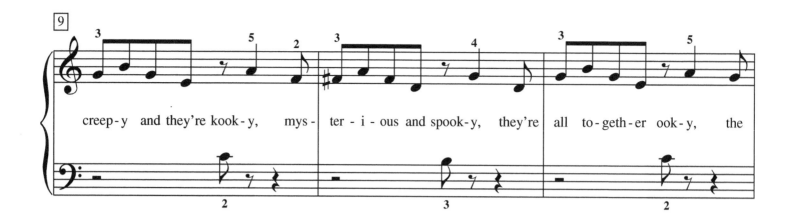

creep-y and they're kook-y, mys- ter - i - ous and spook-y, they're all to-geth-er ook-y, the

Ad-dams Fam - i - ly. Their house is a mu-se-um, where peo-ple come to see 'em. They

real-ly are a scree-um, the Ad-dams Fam-i - ly. *mf* *(Spoken:) Neat.*

Sweet.   Petite.   So

get a witch-'s shawl on,   a broom-stick you can crawl on,   we're

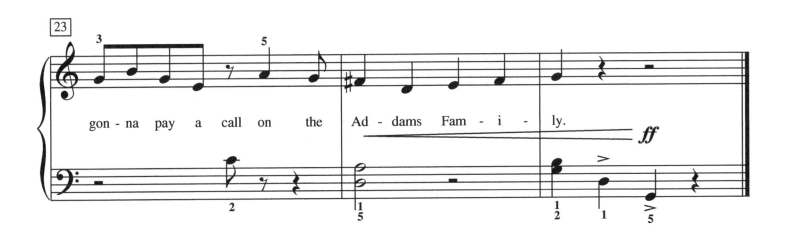

gon-na pay a call on the Ad - dams Fam - i - ly.

9

Little Shop of Horrors

from the Stage Production LITTLE SHOP OF HORRORS

Words by Howard Ashman
Music by Alan Menken
Arranged by Fred Kern

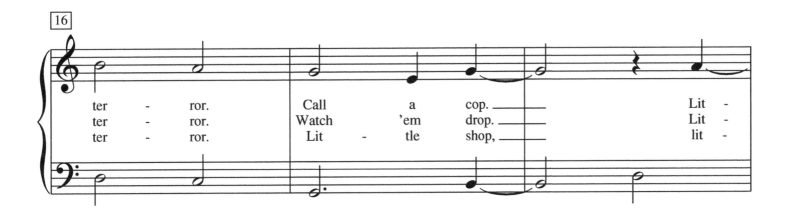

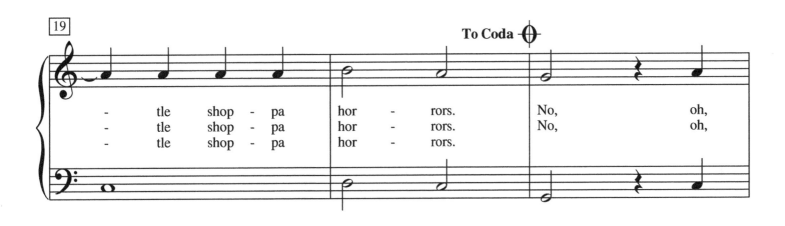

ling, what a creep - y thing to be

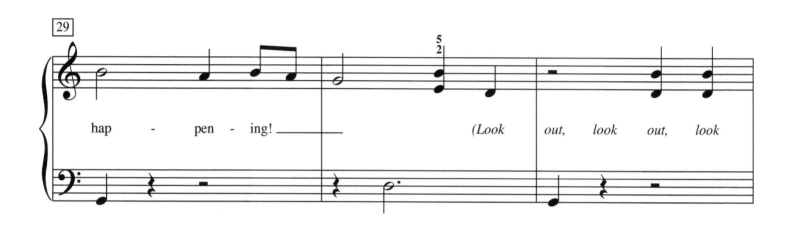

hap - pen - ing! _____ (Look out, look out, look

out, look out!) *mf* Shang - a - lang, feel ___

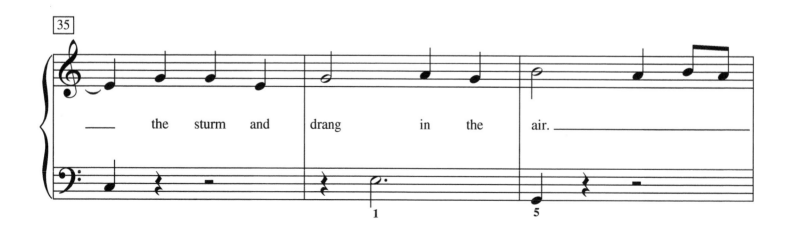

___ the sturm and drang in the air. _____

(Yeah, _____ yeah, _____ yeah.)

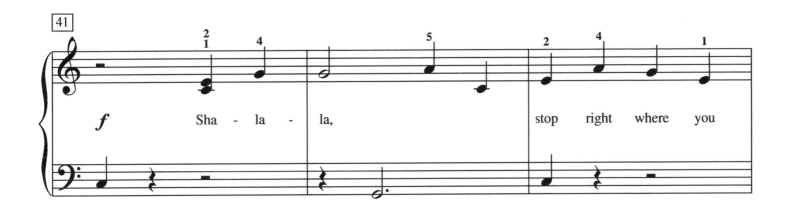

f   Sha - la - la,   stop right where you

are. Don't   move   a   thing. _____

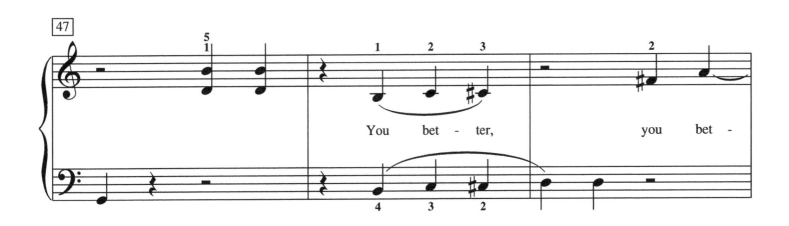

You bet - ter,   you bet -

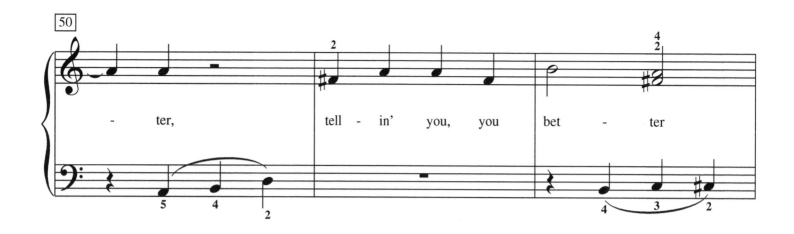

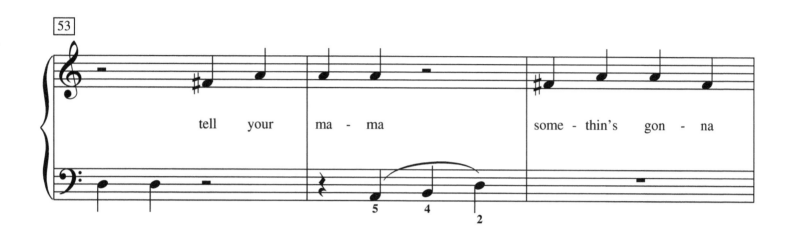

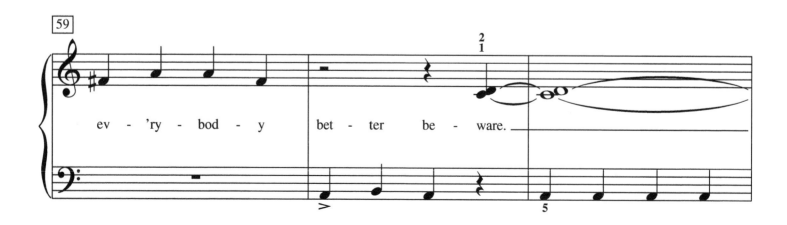

14

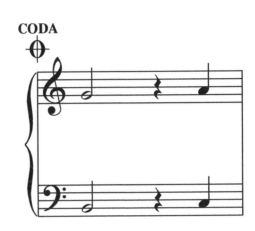

(Com - ma, com - ma, com - ma)

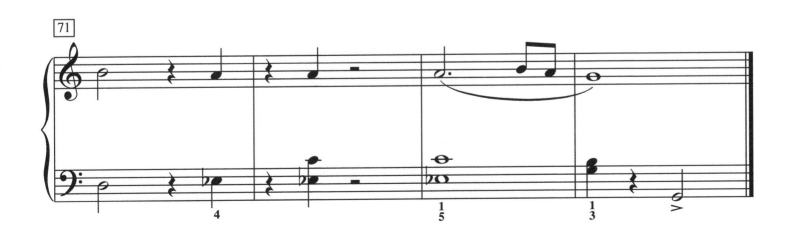

Monster's Holiday

Words and Music by
Buck Owens
Arranged by Fred Kern

Moderately (♩ = 142)

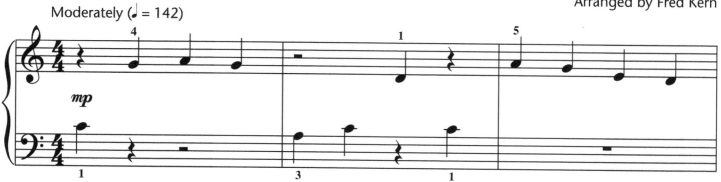

Frank - en - stein was the first in line ___ and the

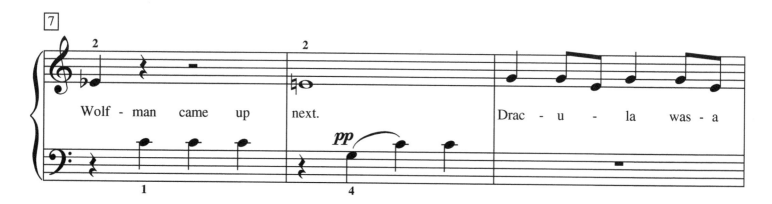

Wolf - man came up next. Drac - u - la was a

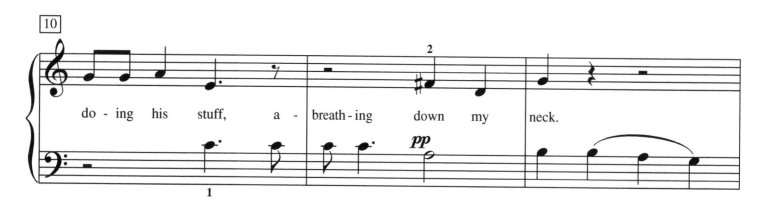

do - ing his stuff, a - breath-ing down my neck.

Jump back, — make tracks, here comes the Hunch - back, bet - ter get out of his

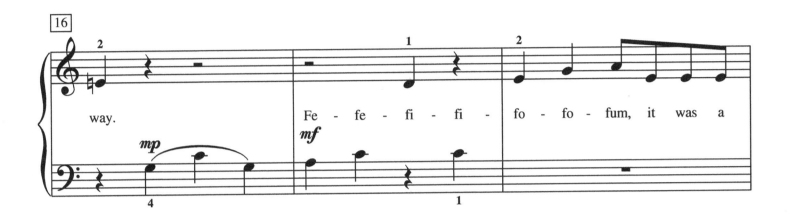

way. Fe - fe - fi - fi - fo - fo - fum, it was a

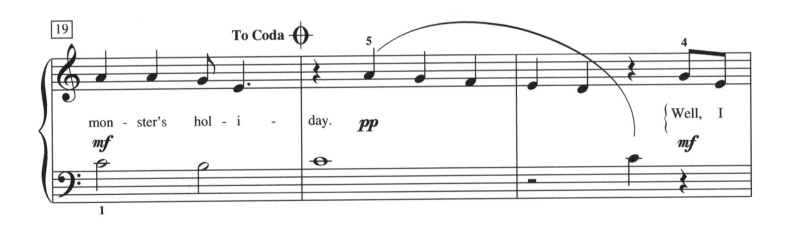

mon - ster's hol - i - day. Well, I

hopped in - to bed and I cov - ered up my head, — said, "I'm
Un - cle — Bill, well, — he — took — ill — and they

gon - na get a good night's sleep." I
sent for _____ me to come. Well, I got woke up a - bout

twelve o' - clock ___ and I jumped right to my feet. There was
the old grave - yard ___ so I went on the run. There was

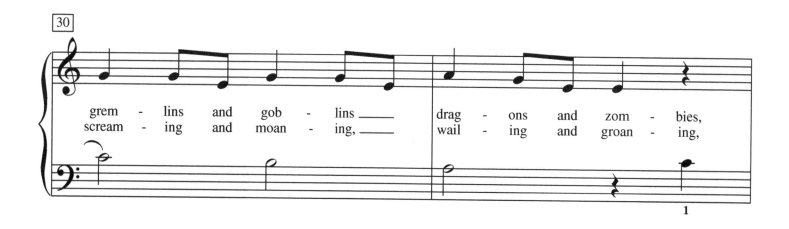

grem - lins and gob - lins ___ drag - ons and zom - bies,
scream - ing and moan - ing, ___ wail - ing and groan - ing,

Lord - y what an aw - ful sight! I said, "Good
scar - y as a mum - my's curse. I said, "Good

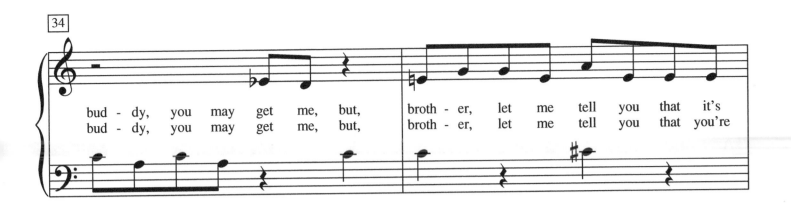

bud - dy, you may get me, but, broth - er, let me tell you that it's
bud - dy, you may get me, but, broth - er, let me tell you that you're

gon - na be af - ter the fight." *mf* first." *mf*
gon - na have to catch __ me

D.S. al Coda

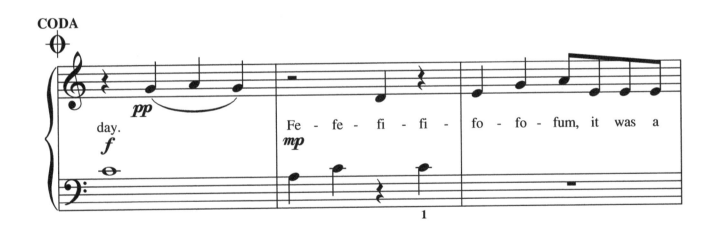

CODA

day. Fe - fe - fi - fi - fo - fo - fum, it was a

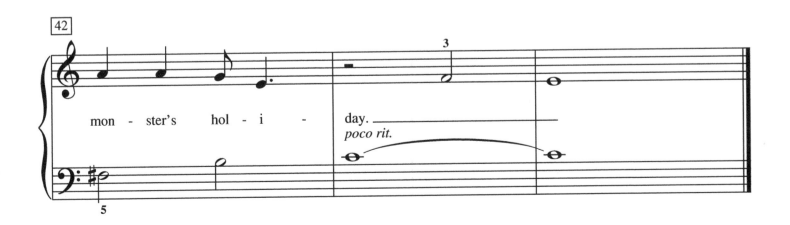

mon - ster's hol - i - day. __

poco rit.

19

Purple People Eater™

Words and Music by
Sheb Wooley®
Arranged by Fred Kern

Bright Rock tempo (♩ = 120)

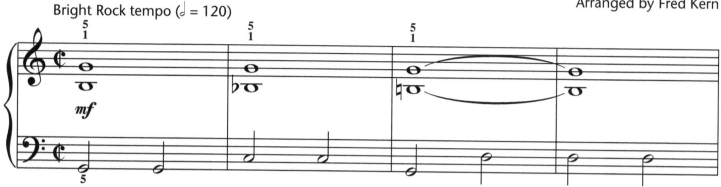

(cross 2 over 1)

1. saw the thing a - com - in' out of the sky. It had
2. came down to earth and he lit in a tree. I said,
3.–5. *(See additional lyrics)*

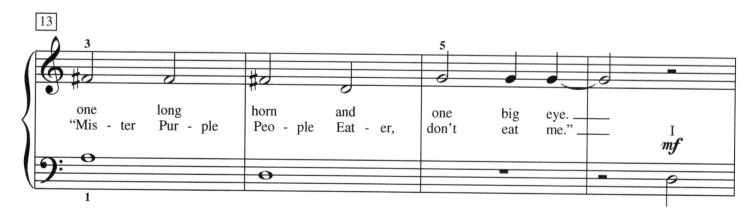

one long horn and one big eye.
"Mis - ter Pur - ple Peo - ple Eat - er, don't eat me." I

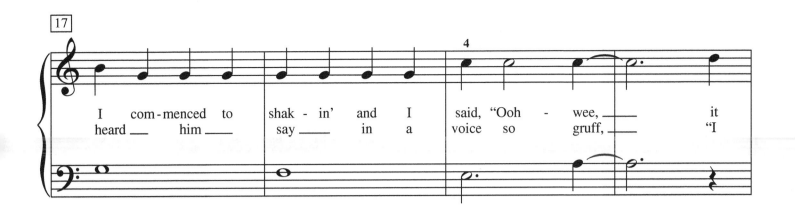

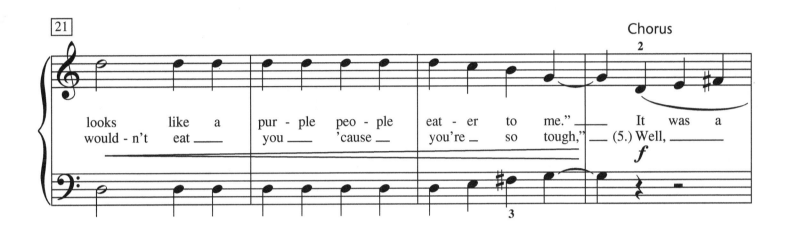

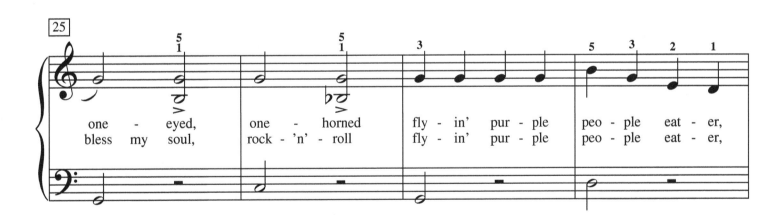

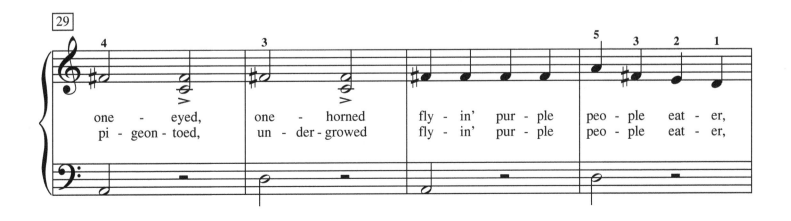

one - eyed, one - horned fly - in' pur - ple peo - ple eat - er, sure looked
he wears short shorts, fly - in' pur - ple peo - ple eat - er. What a

strange to me.
sight to see.

2. Well, he
mp

(cross 2 over 1)

mp

Additional Lyrics

3. I said, "Mister purple people eater, what's your line?"
He said, "Eatin' purple people, and it sure is fine,
But that's not the reason that I came to land,
I wanna get a job in a rock and roll band."
Chorus

4. And then he swung from the tree and he lit on the ground,
And he started to rock, a-really rockin' around.
It was a crazy ditty with a swingin' tune,
Singa bop bapa loop a lap a loom bam boom.
Chorus

5. Well, he went on his way and then what-a you know,
I saw him last night on a TV show,
He was blowin' it out, really knockin' 'em dead,
Playin' rock 'n' roll music thru the horn in his head.
Chorus

(Ghost)
Riders in the Sky
(A Cowboy Legend)
from RIDERS IN THE SKY

By Stan Jones
Arranged by Fred Kern

Mysteriously (♩ = 100)

An old cow - poke went rid - ing out one
horns are black and shin - y and their

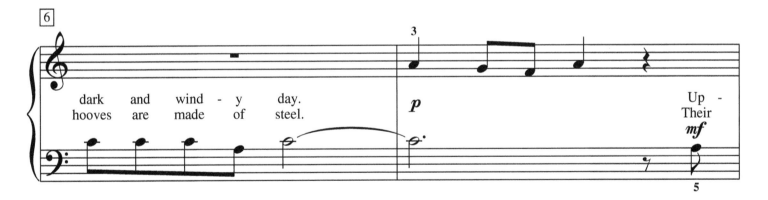

dark and wind - y day.
hooves are made of steel.

Up -
Their

Accompaniment (Student plays one octave higher than written.)

Mysteriously (♩ = 100)

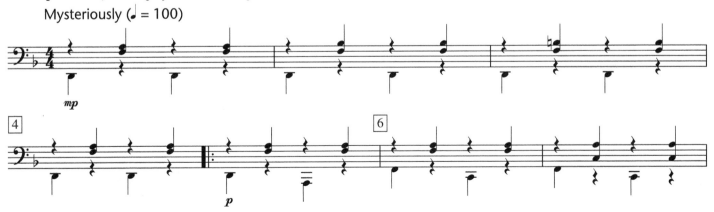

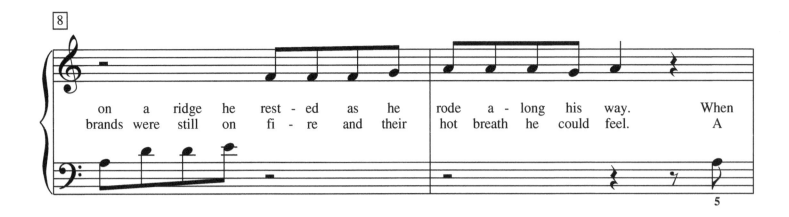

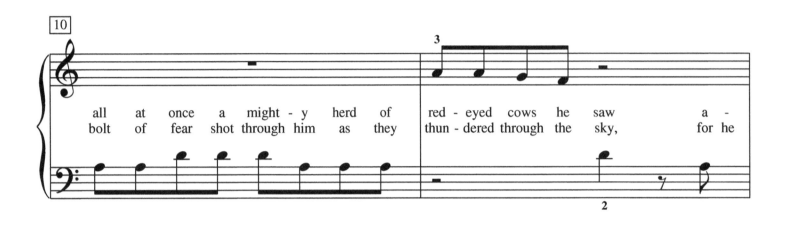

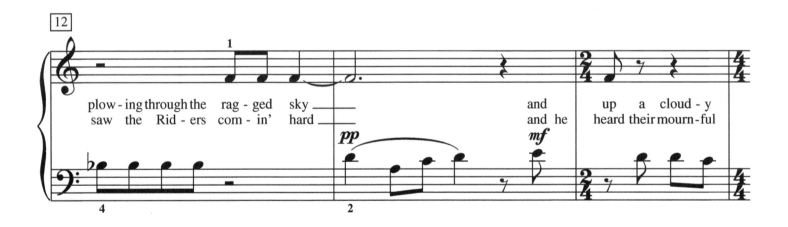

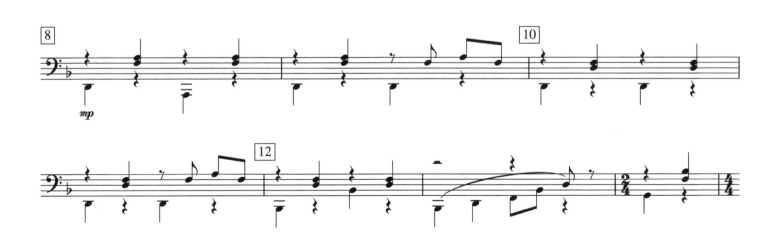

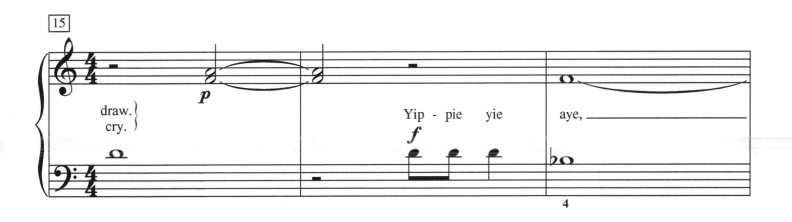

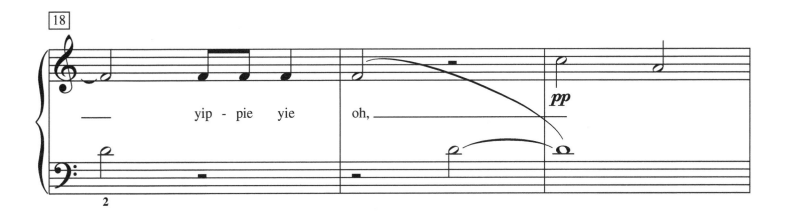

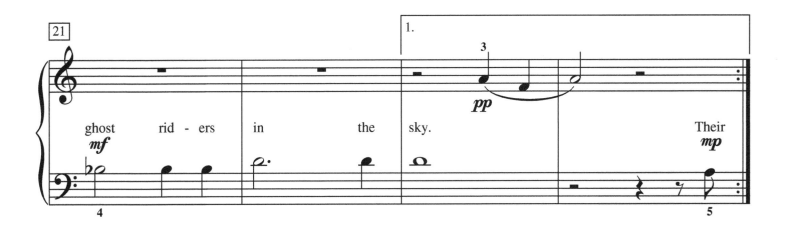

sky.
As the rid - ers loped on by him, he

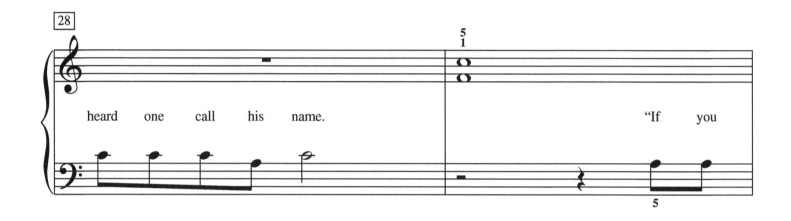

heard one call his name.
"If you

want to save your soul from Hell a - rid - in' on our range, then

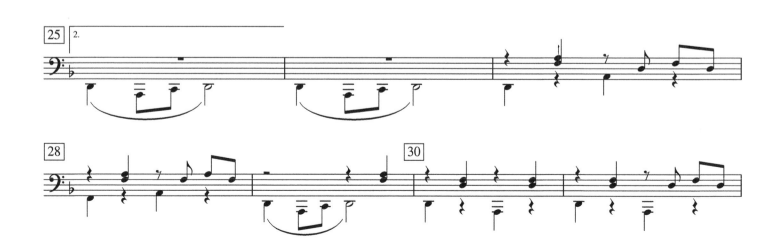

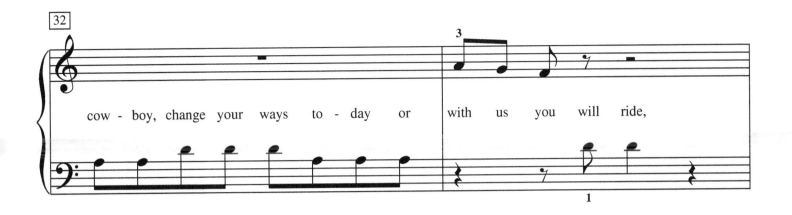

cow - boy, change your ways to - day or with us you will ride,

tryin' to catch the Dev - il's herd _____ a -

cross these end - less skies." Yip - pie yie

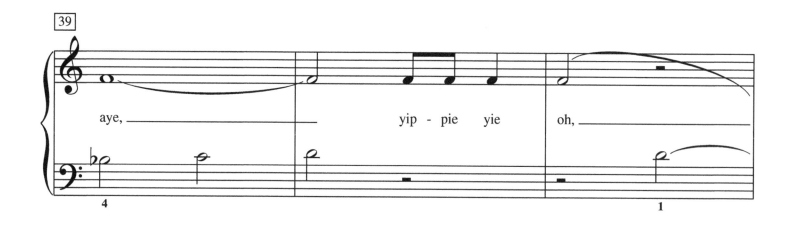

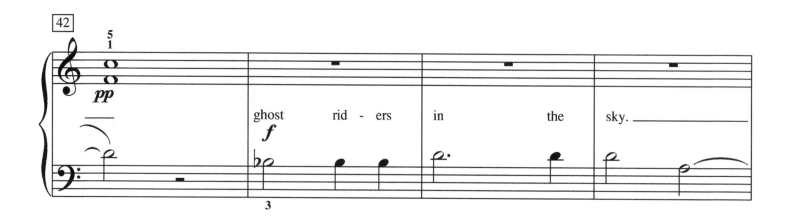

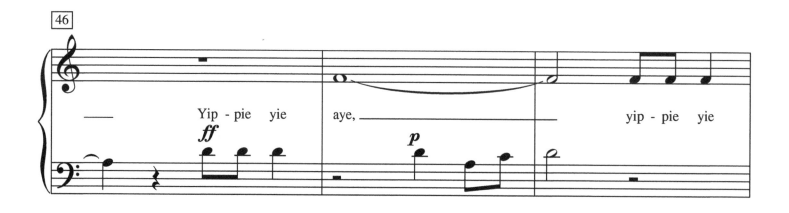

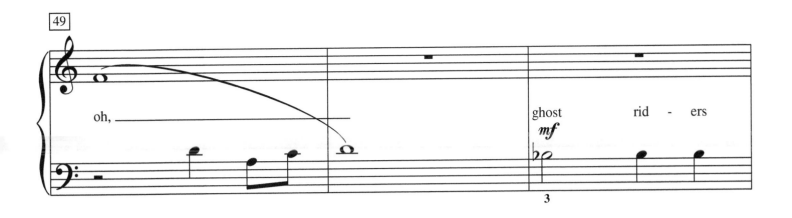

oh, _____

ghost rid - ers

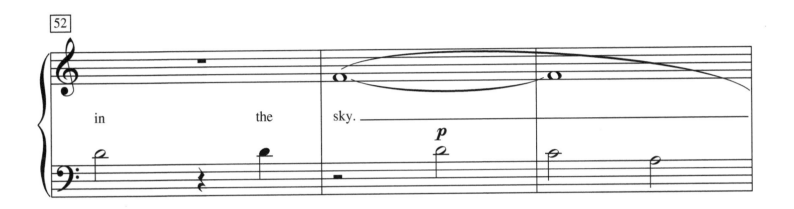

in the sky. _____

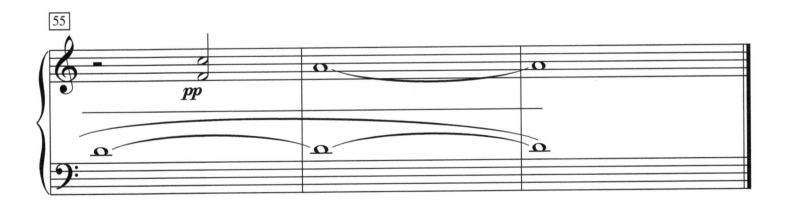

Song of the Volga Boatman

Russian Folk Song
Arranged by Fred Kern

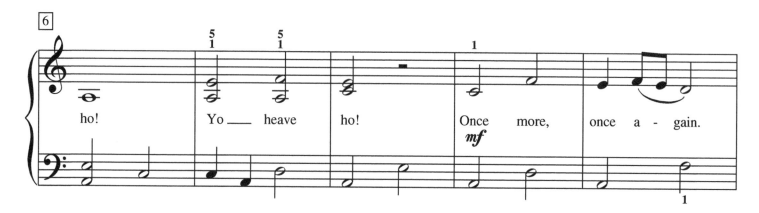

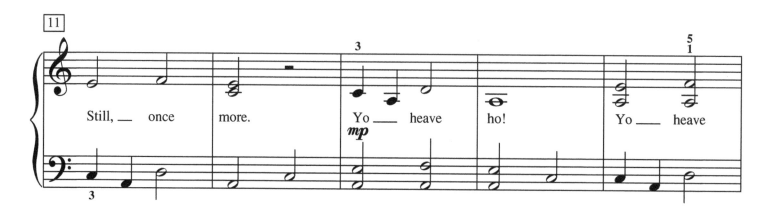

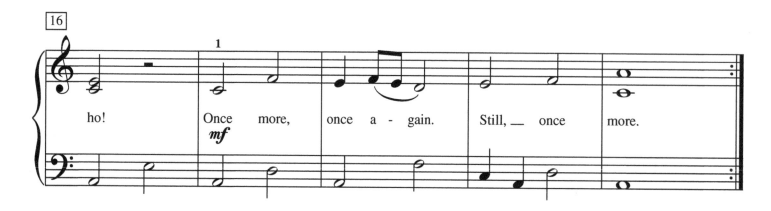

This Is Halloween

from Tim Burton's THE NIGHTMARE BEFORE CHRISTMAS

Music and Lyrics by
Danny Elfman
Arranged by Fred Kern

Pump - kins scream in the dead of night! This is Hal - low - een,

mf

(cross 2 over 1)

ev - 'ry - bod - y make a scene. Trick or treat 'til they die of fright.

This is Hal - low - een!

f

mf

Ten - der lump - lings ev - er - y - where. Life's no fun with - out a good scare.

mp

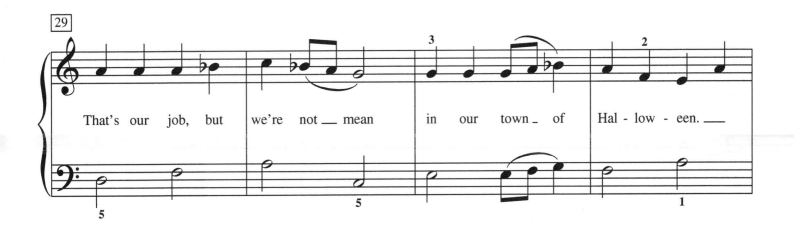

Lyrics: That's our job, but we're not mean in our town of Hal - low - een.

Lyrics: In this town that we call home ev - 'ry - one hail to the

Lyrics: Pump - kin Song! This is Hal - low - een! This is

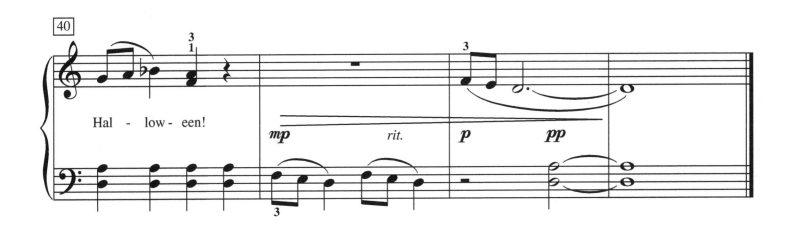

Lyrics: Hal - low - een!

The Thing

Words and Music by
Charles R. Grean
Arranged by Fred Kern

Brightly (♩ = 190)

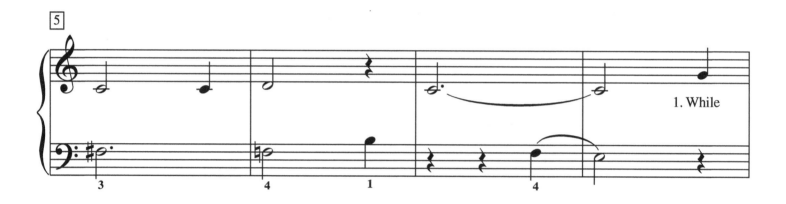

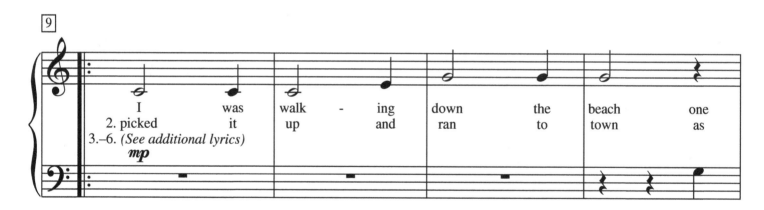

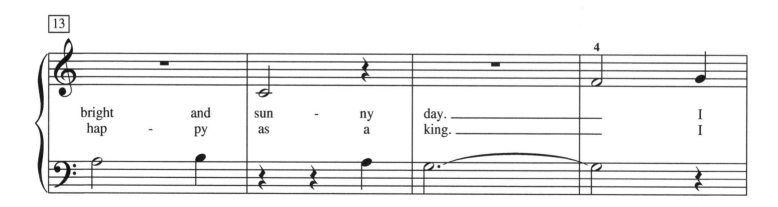

saw a great big wood - en box a -
took it to a guy I know who'd

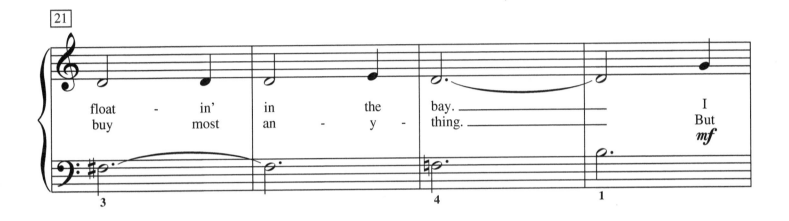

float - in' in the bay. I
buy most an - y - thing. But

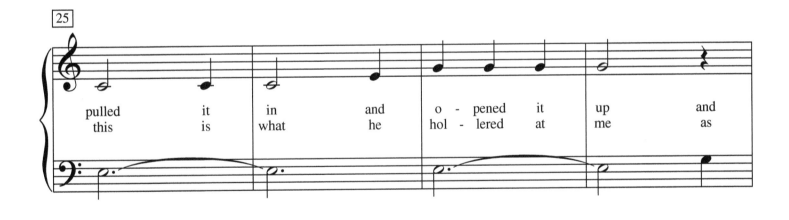

pulled it in and o - pened it up and
this is what he hol - lered at me as

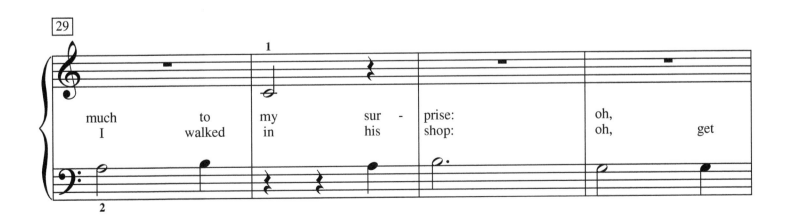

much to my sur - prise: oh,
I walked in his shop: oh, get

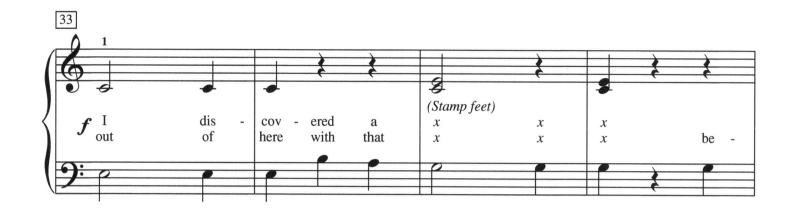

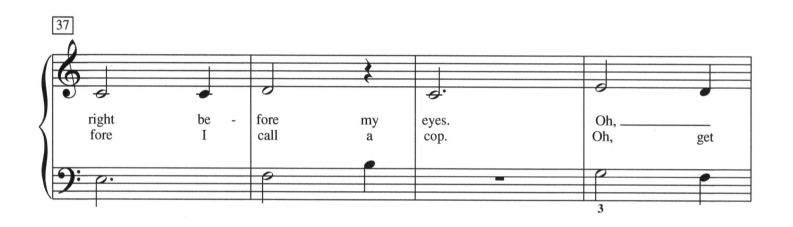

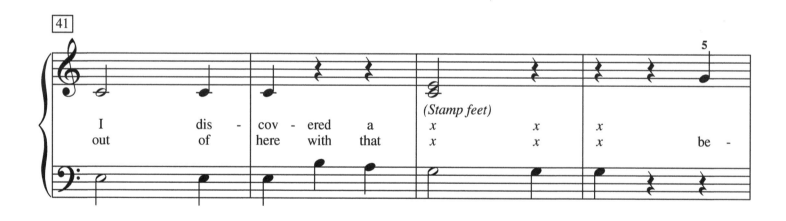

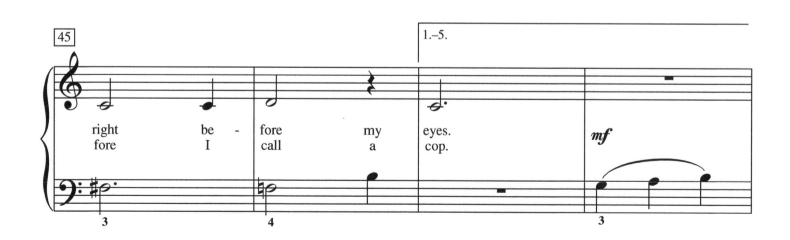

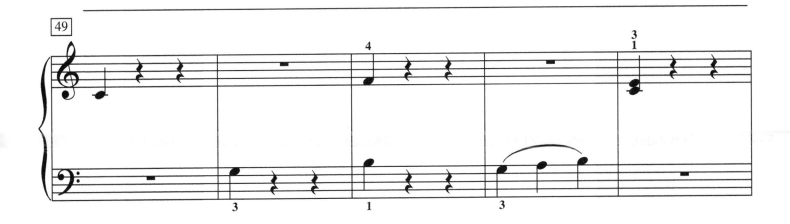

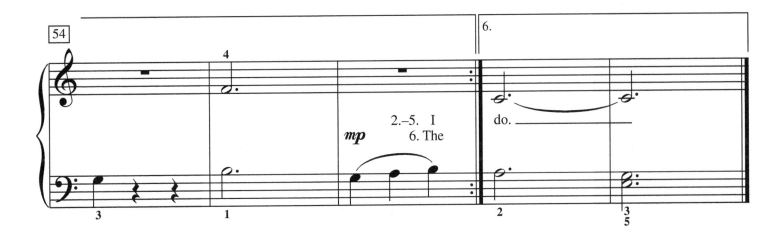

Additional Lyrics

3. I turned and got right out a-runnin' for my life,
   And then I took it home with me to give it to my wife.
   But this is what she hollered at me as I walked in the door:
   Oh, get out of here with that xxx and don't come back no more.
   Oh, get out of here with that xxx and don't come back no more.

4. I wandered all around the town until I chanced to meet
   A hobo who was looking for a handout on the street.
   He said he'd take most any old thing, he was a desperate man,
   But when I showed him the xxx, he turned around and ran.
   Oh, when I showed him the xxx, he turned around and ran.

5. I wandered on for many years, a victim of my fate,
   Until one day I came upon Saint Peter at the gate.
   And when I tried to take it inside he told me where to go:
   Get out of here with that xxx and take it down below.
   Oh, get out of here with that xxx and take it down below.

6. The moral of the story is if you're out on the beach
   And you should see a great big box and it's within your reach,
   Don't ever stop and open it up, that's my advice to you,
   'Cause you'll never get rid of the xxx, no matter what you do.
   Oh, you'll never get rid of the xxx, no matter what you do.

COMPOSER SHOWCASE
HAL LEONARD STUDENT PIANO LIBRARY

This series showcases great original piano music from our **Hal Leonard Student Piano Library** family of composers. Carefully graded for easy selection.

BILL BOYD

JAZZ BITS (AND PIECES)
Early Intermediate Level
00290312 11 Solos......................$7.99

JAZZ DELIGHTS
Intermediate Level
00240435 11 Solos......................$8.99

JAZZ FEST
Intermediate Level
00240436 10 Solos......................$8.99

JAZZ PRELIMS
Early Elementary Level
00290032 12 Solos......................$7.99

JAZZ SKETCHES
Intermediate Level
00220001 8 Solos......................$8.99

JAZZ STARTERS
Elementary Level
00290425 10 Solos......................$8.99

JAZZ STARTERS II
Late Elementary Level
00290434 11 Solos......................$7.99

JAZZ STARTERS III
Late Elementary Level
00290465 12 Solos......................$8.99

THINK JAZZ!
Early Intermediate Level
00290417 Method Book...........$12.99

TONY CARAMIA

JAZZ MOODS
Intermediate Level
00296728 8 Solos......................$6.95

SUITE DREAMS
Intermediate Level
00296775 4 Solos......................$6.99

SONDRA CLARK

DAKOTA DAYS
Intermediate Level
00296521 5 Solos......................$6.95

FLORIDA FANTASY SUITE
Intermediate Level
00296766 3 Duets......................$7.95

THREE ODD METERS
Intermediate Level
00296472 3 Duets......................$6.95

MATTHEW EDWARDS

CONCERTO FOR YOUNG PIANISTS
FOR 2 PIANOS, FOUR HANDS
Intermediate Level Book/CD
00296356 3 Movements $19.99

CONCERTO NO. 2 IN G MAJOR
FOR 2 PIANOS, 4 HANDS
Intermediate Level Book/CD
00296670 3 Movements...........$17.99

PHILLIP KEVEREN

MOUSE ON A MIRROR
Late Elementary Level
00296361 5 Solos......................$8.99

MUSICAL MOODS
Elementary/Late Elementary Level
00296714 7 Solos......................$6.99

SHIFTY-EYED BLUES
Late Elementary Level
00296374 5 Solos......................$7.99

CAROL KLOSE

THE BEST OF CAROL KLOSE
Early to Late Intermediate Level
00146151 15 Solos....................$12.99

CORAL REEF SUITE
Late Elementary Level
00296354 7 Solos......................$7.50

DESERT SUITE
Intermediate Level
00296667 6 Solos......................$7.99

FANCIFUL WALTZES
Early Intermediate Level
00296473 5 Solos......................$7.95

GARDEN TREASURES
Late Intermediate Level
00296787 5 Solos......................$8.50

ROMANTIC EXPRESSIONS
Intermediate to Late Intermediate Level
00296923 5 Solos......................$8.99

WATERCOLOR MINIATURES
Early Intermediate Level
00296848 7 Solos......................$7.99

JENNIFER LINN

AMERICAN IMPRESSIONS
Intermediate Level
00296471 6 Solos......................$8.99

ANIMALS HAVE FEELINGS TOO
Early Elementary/Elementary Level
00147789 8 Solos......................$8.99

AU CHOCOLAT
Late Elementary/Early Intermediate Level
00298110 7 Solos......................$8.99

CHRISTMAS IMPRESSIONS
Intermediate Level
00296706 8 Solos......................$8.99

JUST PINK
Elementary Level
00296722 9 Solos......................$8.99

LES PETITES IMAGES
Late Elementary Level
00296664 7 Solos......................$8.99

LES PETITES IMPRESSIONS
Intermediate Level
00296355 6 Solos......................$8.99

REFLECTIONS
Late Intermediate Level
00296843 5 Solos......................$8.99

TALES OF MYSTERY
Intermediate Level
00296769 6 Solos......................$8.99

LYNDA LYBECK-ROBINSON

ALASKA SKETCHES
Early Intermediate Level
00119637 8 Solos......................$8.99

AN AWESOME ADVENTURE
Late Elementary Level
00137563 8 Solos......................$7.99

FOR THE BIRDS
Early Intermediate/Intermediate Level
00237078 9 Solos......................$8.99

WHISPERING WOODS
Late Elementary Level
00275905 9 Solos......................$8.99

MONA REJINO

CIRCUS SUITE
Late Elementary Level
00296665 5 Solos......................$8.99

COLOR WHEEL
Early Intermediate Level
00201951 6 Solos......................$9.99

IMPRESIONES DE ESPAÑA
Intermediate Level
00337520 6 Solos......................$8.99

IMPRESSIONS OF NEW YORK
Intermediate Level
00364212......................$8.99

JUST FOR KIDS
Elementary Level
00296840 8 Solos......................$7.99

MERRY CHRISTMAS MEDLEYS
Intermediate Level
00296799 5 Solos......................$8.99

MINIATURES IN STYLE
Intermediate Level
00148088 6 Solos......................$8.99

PORTRAITS IN STYLE
Early Intermediate Level
00296507 6 Solos......................$8.99

EUGÉNIE ROCHEROLLE

CELEBRATION SUITE
Intermediate Level
00152724 3 Duets......................$8.99

ENCANTOS ESPAÑOLES (SPANISH DELIGHTS)
Intermediate Level
00125451 6 Solos......................$8.99

JAMBALAYA
Intermediate Level
00296654 2 Pianos, 8 Hands.....$12.99
00296725 2 Pianos, 4 Hands.......$7.95

JEROME KERN CLASSICS
Intermediate Level
00296577 10 Solos....................$12.99

LITTLE BLUES CONCERTO
Early Intermediate Level
00142801 2 Pianos, 4 Hands......$12.99

TOUR FOR TWO
Late Elementary Level
00296832 6 Duets......................$9.99

TREASURES
Late Elementary/Early Intermediate Level
00296924 7 Solos......................$8.99

JEREMY SISKIND

BIG APPLE JAZZ
Intermediate Level
00278209 8 Solos......................$8.99

MYTHS AND MONSTERS
Late Elementary/Early Intermediate Level
00148148 9 Solos......................$8.99

CHRISTOS TSITSAROS

DANCES FROM AROUND THE WORLD
Early Intermediate Level
00296688 7 Solos......................$8.99

FIVE SUMMER PIECES
Late Intermediate/Advanced Level
00361235 5 Solos......................$12.99

LYRIC BALLADS
Intermediate/Late Intermediate Level
00102404 6 Solos......................$8.99

POETIC MOMENTS
Intermediate Level
00296403 8 Solos......................$8.99

SEA DIARY
Early Intermediate Level
00253486 9 Solos......................$8.99

SONATINA HUMORESQUE
Late Intermediate Level
00296772 3 Movements.............$6.99

SONGS WITHOUT WORDS
Intermediate Level
00296506 9 Solos......................$9.99

THREE PRELUDES
Early Advanced Level
00130747 3 Solos......................$8.99

THROUGHOUT THE YEAR
Late Elementary Level
00296723 12 Duets....................$6.95

ADDITIONAL COLLECTIONS

AT THE LAKE
by Elvina Pearce
Elementary/Late Elementary Level
00131642 10 Solos and Duets.....$7.99

CHRISTMAS FOR TWO
by Dan Fox
Early Intermediate Level
00290069 13 Duets....................$8.99

CHRISTMAS JAZZ
by Mike Springer
Intermediate Level
00296525 6 Solos......................$8.99

COUNTY RAGTIME FESTIVAL
by Fred Kern
Intermediate Level
00296882 7 Solos......................$7.99

LITTLE JAZZERS
by Jennifer Watts
Elementary/Late Elementary Level
00154573 9 Solos......................$8.99

PLAY THE BLUES!
by Luann Carman
Early Intermediate Level
00296357 10 Solos....................$9.99

ROLLER COASTERS & RIDES
by Jennifer & Mike Watts
Intermediate Level
00131144 8 Duets......................$8.99

HAL•LEONARD®
www.halleonard.com

Prices, contents, and availability subject
to change without notice.

POPULAR SONGS
HAL LEONARD STUDENT PIANO LIBRARY

The **Hal Leonard Student Piano Library** has great songs, and you will find all your favorites here: Disney classics, Broadway and movie favorites, and today's top hits. These graded collections are skillfully and imaginatively arranged for students and pianists at every level, from elementary solos with teacher accompaniments to sophisticated piano solos for the advancing pianist.

Adele
arr. Mona Rejino
Correlates with HLSPL Level 5
00159590.............................$12.99

The Beatles
arr. Eugénie Rocherolle
Correlates with HLSPL Level 5
00296649............................. $12.99

Irving Berlin Piano Duos
arr. Don Heitler and Jim Lyke
Correlates with HLSPL Level 5
00296838.............................$14.99

Broadway Favorites
arr. Phillip Keveren
Correlates with HLSPL Level 4
00279192.............................$12.99

Chart Hits
arr. Mona Rejino
Correlates with HLSPL Level 5
00296710.............................$8.99

Christmas at the Piano
arr. Lynda Lybeck-Robinson
Correlates with HLSPL Level 4
00298194.............................$12.99

Christmas Cheer
arr. Phillip Keveren
Correlates with HLSPL Level 4
00296616.............................$8.99

Classic Christmas Favorites
arr. Jennifer & Mike Watts
Correlates with HLSPL Level 5
00129582.............................$9.99

Christmas Time Is Here
arr. Eugénie Rocherolle
Correlates with HLSPL Level 5
00296614.............................$8.99

Classic Joplin Rags
arr. Fred Kern
Correlates with HLSPL Level 5
00296743.............................$9.99

Classical Pop – Lady Gaga Fugue & Other Pop Hits
arr. Giovanni Dettori
Correlates with HLSPL Level 5
00296921.............................$12.99

Contemporary Movie Hits
arr. by Carol Klose, Jennifer Linn and Wendy Stevens
Correlates with HLSPL Level 5
00296780.............................$8.99

Contemporary Pop Hits
arr. Wendy Stevens
Correlates with HLSPL Level 3
00296836.............................$8.99

Cool Pop
arr. Mona Rejino
Correlates with HLSPL Level 5
00360103.............................$12.99

Country Favorites
arr. Mona Rejino
Correlates with HLSPL Level 5
00296861.............................$9.99

Disney Favorites
arr. Phillip Keveren
Correlates with HLSPL Levels 3/4
00296647.............................$10.99

Disney Film Favorites
arr. Mona Rejino
Correlates with HLSPL Level 5
00296809 ....$10.99

Disney Piano Duets
arr. Jennifer & Mike Watts
Correlates with HLSPL Level 5
00113759.............................$13.99

Double Agent! Piano Duets
arr. Jeremy Siskind
Correlates with HLSPL Level 5
00121595.............................$12.99

Easy Christmas Duets
arr. Mona Rejino & Phillip Keveren
Correlates with HLSPL Levels 3/4
00237139.............................$9.99

Easy Disney Duets
arr. Jennifer and Mike Watts
Correlates with HLSPL Level 4
00243727.............................$12.99

Four Hands on Broadway
arr. Fred Kern
Correlates with HLSPL Level 5
00146177.............................$12.99

Frozen Piano Duets
arr. Mona Rejino
Correlates with HLSPL Levels 3/4
00144294.............................$12.99

Hip-Hop for Piano Solo
arr. Logan Evan Thomas
Correlates with HLSPL Level 5
00360950.............................$12.99

Jazz Hits for Piano Duet
arr. Jeremy Siskind
Correlates with HLSPL Level 5
00143248.............................$12.99

Elton John
arr. Carol Klose
Correlates with HLSPL Level 5
00296721.............................$10.99

Joplin Ragtime Duets
arr. Fred Kern
Correlates with HLSPL Level 5
00296771.............................$8.99

Movie Blockbusters
arr. Mona Rejino
Correlates with HLSPL Level 5
00232850.............................$10.99

The Nutcracker Suite
arr. Lynda Lybeck-Robinson
Correlates with HLSPL Levels 3/4
00147906.............................$8.99

Pop Hits for Piano Duet
arr. Jeremy Siskind
Correlates with HLSPL Level 5
00224734.............................$12.99

Sing to the King
arr. Phillip Keveren
Correlates with HLSPL Level 5
00296808.............................$8.99

Smash Hits
arr. Mona Rejino
Correlates with HLSPL Level 5
00284841.............................$10.99

Spooky Halloween Tunes
arr. Fred Kern
Correlates with HLSPL Levels 3/4
00121550.............................$9.99

Today's Hits
arr. Mona Rejino
Correlates with HLSPL Level 5
00296646.............................$9.99

Top Hits
arr. Jennifer and Mike Watts
Correlates with HLSPL Level 5
00296894.............................$10.99

Top Piano Ballads
arr. Jennifer Watts
Correlates with HLSPL Level 5
00197926.............................$10.99

Video Game Hits
arr. Mona Rejino
Correlates with HLSPL Level 4
00300310.............................$12.99

You Raise Me Up
arr. Deborah Brady
Correlates with HLSPL Level 2/3
00296576.............................$7.95

HAL•LEONARD®
7777 W. BLUEMOUND RD. P.O. BOX 13819 MILWAUKEE, WI 53213

Visit our website at **www.halleonard.com**

Piano Recital Showcase

"What should my students play for the recital?" This series provides easy answers to this common question. For these winning collections, we've carefully selected some of the most popular and effective pieces from the **Hal Leonard Student Library** – from early-elementary to late-intermediate levels. You'll love the variety of musical styles found in each book.

PIANO RECITAL SHOWCASE PRE-STAFF
Pre-Staff Early Elementary Level
8 solos: Bumper Cars • Cherokee Lullaby • Fire Dance • The Hungry Spider • On a Magic Carpet • One, Two, Three • Pickled Pepper Polka • Pumpkin Song.
00296784 ....$7.99

BOOK 1
Elementary Level
12 solos: B.B.'s Boogie • In My Dreams • Japanese Garden • Jazz Jig • Joyful Bells • Lost Treasure • Monster March • Ocean Breezes • Party Cat Parade • Rainy Day Play • Sledding Fun • Veggie Song.
00296749 ....$8.99

BOOK 2
Late-Elementary Level
12 solos: Angelfish Arabesque • The Brontosaurus Bop • From the Land of Make-Believe • Ghosts of a Sunken Pirate Ship • The Happy Walrus • Harvest Dance • Hummingbird (L'oiseau-mouche) • Little Bird • Quick Spin in a Fast Car • Shifty-Eyed Blues • The Snake Charmer • Soft Shoe Shuffle.
00296748 ....$8.99

BOOK 3
Intermediate Level
10 solos: Castilian Dreamer • Dreaming Song • Jump Around Rag • Little Mazurka • Meaghan's Melody • Mountain Splendor • Seaside Stride • Snap to It! • Too Cool to Fool • Wizard's Wish.
00296747 ....$8.99

BOOK 4
Late-Intermediate Level
8 solos: Berceuse for Janey • Cafe Waltz • Forever in My Heart • Indigo Bay • Salsa Picante • Sassy Samba • Skater's Dream • Twilight on the Lake.
00296746 ....$8.99

CHRISTMAS EVE SOLOS
Intermediate Level
Composed for the intermediate level student, these pieces provide fresh and substantial repertoire for students not quite ready for advanced piano literature. Includes: Auld Lang Syne • Bring a Torch, Jeannette, Isabella • Coventry Carol • O Little Town of Bethlehem • Silent Night • We Wish You a Merry Christmas • and more.
00296877...$8.99

DUET FAVORITES
Intermediate Level
Five original duets for one piano, four hands from top composers Phillip Keveren, Eugénie Rocherolle, Sondra Clark and Wendy Stevens. Includes: Angel Falls • Crescent City Connection • Prime Time • A Wind of Promise • Yearning.
00296898...$9.99

FESTIVAL FAVORITES, BOOK 1
10 OUTSTANDING NFMC SELECTED SOLOS
Late Elementary/Early Intermediate Level
Proven piano solos fill this compilation of selected gems chosen for various National Federation of Music Clubs (NFMC) Junior Festival lists. Titles: Candlelight Prelude • Crazy Man's Blues • I've Gotta Toccata • Pagoda Bells • Tarantella • Toccata Festivo • Tonnerre sur les plaines (Thunder on the Plains) • Twister • Way Cool! • Wild Robot.
00118198...$10.99

FESTIVAL FAVORITES, BOOK 2
10 OUTSTANDING NFMC SELECTED SOLOS
Intermediate/Late Intermediate Level
Book 2 features: Barcarolle Impromptu • Cathedral Echoes (Harp Song) • Dance of the Trolls • Jasmine in the Mist • Jesters • Maestro, There's a Fly in My Waltz • Mother Earth, Sister Moon • Northwoods Toccata • Sounds of the Rain • Un phare dans le brouillard (A Lighthouse in the Fog).
00118202...$10.99

FESTIVAL GEMS – BOOK 1
Elementary/Late Elementary Level
This convenient collection features 10 NFMC-selected piano solos: Brooklyn's Waltz • Chimichanga Cha-Cha • Feelin' Happy • Footprints in the Snow • Lazy Daisy • New Orleans Jamboree • PBJ Blues • Pepperoni Pizza • Sneakin' Cake • Things That Go Bump in the Night. (Note: Solos are from previous NFMC lists.)
00193548 ....$10.99

HAL•LEONARD®

Visit our website at
www.halleonard.com/hlspl
for all the newest titles in this series and other books in the Hal Leonard Student Piano Library.

FESTIVAL GEMS – BOOK 2
Early Intermediate/Intermediate Level
Book 2 includes: Caravan • Chatterbox • In the Groove • Jubilation! • Kokopelli (Invention in Phrygian Mode) • La marée de soir (Evening Tide) • Reverie • Time Travel • Voiliers dans le vent (Sailboats in the Wind) • Williwaw.
00193587 ....$10.99

FESTIVAL GEMS – BOOK 3
Late Intermediate/Early Advanced Level
8 more NFMC-selected piano solos, including: Cuentos Del Matador (Tales of the Matador) • Daffodil Caprice • Love Song in the Rain • Midnight Prayer • Nocturne d'Esprit • Rapsodie • Scherzo • Urban Heartbeat.
00193588 ....$10.99

RAGTIME!
Early Intermediate/Intermediate Level
8 original rags from Bill Boyd, Phillip Keveren, Carol Klose, Jennifer Linn, Mona Rejino, Christos Tsitsaros and Jennifer & Mike Watts are featured in this solo piano collection. Includes: Butterfly Rag • Carnival Rag • Jump Around Rag • Nashville Rag • Ragtime Blue • St. Louis Rag • Swingin' Rag • Techno Rag.
00124242 ....$9.99

ROMANTIC INSPIRATIONS
Early Advanced Level
From "Arabesque" to "Nocturne" to "Rapsodie," the inspired pieces in this collection are a perfect choice for students who want to play beautiful, expressive and impressive literature at the recital. Includes: Arabesque • Journey's End • Nocturne • Nocturne d'Esprit • Prelude No. 1 • Rapsodie • Rondo Capriccioso • Valse d'Automne.
00296813...$8.99

SUMMERTIME FUN
Elementary Level
Twelve terrific originals from favorite HLSPL composers, all at the elementary level. Songs: Accidental Wizard • Butterflies and Rainbows • Chill Out! • Down by the Lake • The Enchanted Mermaid • Gone Fishin' • The Merry Merry-Go-Round • Missing You • Pink Lemonade • Rockin' the Boat • Teeter-Totter • Wind Chimes.
00296831 ....$7.99

Prices, content, and availability subject to change without notice.

0518